William

Walton

T0071057

Coronation Te Deum

Edited by Timothy Brown

vocal score

Composed for the coronation of HER MAJESTY QUEEN ELIZABETH II
in Westminster Abbey on Tuesday, 2 June 1953

MUSIC DEPARTMENT

OXFORD
UNIVERSITY PRESS

OXFORD
UNIVERSITY PRESS

Great Clarendon Street, Oxford OX2 6DP,
United Kingdom

Oxford University Press is a department of the University of Oxford.
It furthers the University's objective of excellence in research, scholarship,
and education by publishing worldwide. Oxford is a registered trade mark of
Oxford University Press in the UK and in certain other countries

ISBN 978–0–19–339512–1

Music origination by Michael Durnin

Printed in Great Britain on acid-free paper by
Halstan & Co. Ltd, Amersham, Bucks.

PREFACE

Since Edward VII's coronation in 1902, it had become the custom to include a setting of the Te Deum in all subsequent ceremonies. In 1952 there was initially some doubt as to which composer would be invited to compose the Te Deum for the coronation of Queen Elizabeth II the following June. Sir William McKie, organist of Westminster Abbey and the coronation's director of music, discussed the project with Sir William Walton, but he also approached Ralph Vaughan Williams. In the event, Vaughan Williams (who had written the Te Deum for George VI's coronation in 1937) declined the invitation and Walton duly received the commission.

The Te Deum was to come at the point of the ceremony when the Queen, newly crowned, prepared to process out of the abbey to greet her subjects. As the order of service put it: 'In the mean time, the Queen, supported as before, the four swords being carried before her, shall descend from her Throne [and] shall proceed in state through the choir and the nave to the west door of the Church, wearing her Crown and bearing in her right hand the Sceptre and in her left hand the Orb.'

Walton worked closely with McKie. He initially suggested a work of 6 to 8 minutes in length, with the possibility of concluding the text at 'And we worship thy name' and adding perhaps an 'Amen'. He added: 'It has struck me that I might want to use the Queen's Trumpeters for an added effect, but it may not be practicable. But just in case could you let me know their number & your views about it[?] It might be overstepping the mark!' McKie replied with customary precision that the length should be 'no longer than necessary, but it must be long enough for you to have freedom to make the work the grand climax of the whole service'. He reminded Walton that the text, if shortened, must conform to liturgical practice, and that it should contain no '"Amen", or addition of any kind'. He requested an organ part, and added that 'it would help if the chorus parts have no undue rhythmic complications; partly because these are not heard in the Abbey— the sound needs plenty of time to unroll, and the clearer the choral texture, the better it carries; partly because most of the choir are church singers, and can do better in a style more nearly what they are accustomed to.'

Walton's own programme note reveals the care that he took with his composition:

A setting of the Te Deum should reflect the jubilant praise of the words [. . .]. The [Coronation] Te Deum is naturally a more extended work, although I think I am right in saying that it is actually shorter than most other modern Te Deums. It is cast for double choir, full orchestra, and organ. The first problem in setting these magnificent words is naturally one of form—how to equate a satisfactory musical shape with the structure of the prayer. [. . .] I have tried to solve the problem by casting my work in three main sections: there is a long opening section, a quite separate middle section, and an abridged recapitulation in which fresh words are set to music that has already been heard. The idea is that praise and prayer should, by being set to the same music, both be made to seem joyful acts of worship. I can see no reason why a prayer that comes from a Christian heart need not be as confident as the voice of praise. Thus the music that you hear at the beginning to the words 'We praise thee, O God, we acknowledge thee to be the Lord' opens the recapitulation accompanying 'O Lord, save thy people and bless thine heritage', and one or two other similar passages will be noticed.

Nevertheless the work has a quiet ending, partly because its place in the coronation service made this advisable, and just as much because it seemed to me effective to repeat the *marcatissimo* shout of 'let me never be confounded', more simply and peacefully. Faith can be expressed with vigour, but it is essentially a peace at heart.

Walton completed the score promptly. By the middle of November 1952 he had nearly completed the Te Deum. On a postcard to Alan Frank (his editor at OUP) he wrote: 'The "De Te" [*sic*] will appear shortly as now about half way in the scoring. Rather good in spite of being liable to break forth into BF [*Belshazzar's Feast*] every now and then.' To Christopher Hassall (librettist of *Troilus and Cressida*) he wrote: 'I've got cracking on the Te Deum. You will like it, I think, and I hope he [McKie?] will too. Lots of counter-tenors and little boys Holy-holying, not to mention all the Queen's Trumpeters and sidedrum[mers].' In mid-December Walton wrote to McKie: 'Though I hesitate to hazard an opinion when I am so near to a work [. . .] I think it is going to be rather splendid. I have made use of the extra brass, but have arranged it so that it can be dispensed with, if impractical for any reason. There is quite an important & indispensable organ part!'

Walton was much gratified by the response that greeted the exuberant first performance of the Coronation Te Deum on 2 June 1953. The music, described by the music critic Frank Howes as 'shatteringly apt', caught the required mood perfectly and the work met with universal acclaim. More than sixty years later, the Te Deum remains fresh and vivid, a highly effective and tightly structured work. It is an undoubted benchmark for anyone faced with the prospect of composing for a similar royal occasion: its blend of solemnity and theatrical splendour strikes a note that is, in its way, unsurpassable.

TIMOTHY BROWN

The present vocal score is based on the full score published in the William Walton Edition, volume 5, *Choral Works with Orchestra* (2009), edited by Timothy Brown.

INSTRUMENTATION

Full orchestra and organ. The triple woodwind may be reduced to double woodwind if necessary. Additional parts for 4 trumpets, 3 trombones, and side drums are optional. Full score and orchestral parts on hire.

Duration: *c.*9 minutes

Coronation Te Deum

WILLIAM WALT(

*Whenever possible, this part should be sung by counter-tenors only.

* Whenever possible, this chorus should be sung by boys only.

14

a tempo animato, come prima

16

*Whenever possible, this chorus should be sung by boys only.

24

* Whenever possible, these parts should be sung by boys only.